When Good People Throw Bad Parties:
A Guide to Party Politics for Hosts and Guests

by Terri Mandell

First House Press

When Good People Throw Bad Parties:
A Guide to Party Politics for Hosts and Guests

by Terri Mandell

Edited by
Mary McDonald Lewis

Cover design by Sam Concialdi
Book design by Jim Mandell

ISBN # 09- 62306274
Mandell, Terri
When Good People Throw Bad Parties:
A Guide to Party Politics for Hosts and Guests

First House Press
11288 Ventura Blvd. # 392 B
Studio City, Ca. 91604
(818) 980-0212

Acknowledgements

Many thanks to:

Sam Concialdi for visual magic; Mary McDonald Lewis for expert editing; Matt Kramer for coming to all my parties; Jim and Donna for boldly posing for the cover; Penny Warner, Jeanne Anne 'O Connor, Syndi Seid and Kay Okrand for their wisdom and experience; and the Mighty Morphin Power Rangers for keeping Danny occupied while I worked.

Special thanks to my husband Jim Mandell, who participated and contributed during the worst of times.

Table of Contents

This book is dedicated to my mother,
Marilyn Rose, the best party-giver I know.

1. Hosts vs. Guests... Who's on First?

Imagine this scenario:

It's Christmas in the suburbs, and you're on your way to Mark and Janelle Walker's annual Christmas bash. All of their successful, glamorous friends will be there, and their house looks beautiful, immaculately clean and lovingly decorated. The buffet is lavish, and the bar is fully stocked with the best of everything.

You arrive about 30 minutes after the appointed time to find the party in full swing. The room is crowded, and everyone appears to be engaged in sparkling conversation. You don't immediately see anyone you recognize, so you look around for your hosts, but they're temporarily unavailable. You realize that you're on your own for now, so you take a deep breath, walk with great determination into the room, and begin trying to meet people.

Most of the guests are locked into small groups talking among themselves, and you don't feel it would be polite to break in, so you hover nearby, feeling awkward and conspicuous. You make a beeline for the bar to get a drink, and a man comes up beside you to get one for himself. You look at him, smile, and then move on. You scan the room for someone to talk to and feel foolish for not having introduced yourself to the man at the bar. An empty space opens up on the couch and you take it, finding yourself seated next to a woman who's chatting with the couple standing in front of her. You sit there waiting to be noticed, but they don't notice you. You 're uncomfortable just sitting there, so after a minute, you get up and walk around some more, hungry for human contact.

Eventually you meet a nice couple, and after a few minutes of small talk, they excuse themselves. Later, you meet a real estate agent who sells property in your neighborhood. You talk about the market for five minutes, and eventually you drift apart. Finally you spot the hosts, and you visit with them for a while, but they soon get distracted by other guests, and you're on your own again.

It continues like this for about 2 hours, by which time you're bored to death, listless from consuming too much alcohol and exhausted from working so hard at socializing. You leave without saying good-bye.

Does any of this sound familiar? When this happens to you, do you blame yourself for being too shy, lacking networking skills, or just plain being a loser?

When a party becomes strained or dull, when guests have to work too hard at meeting one another, it's usually because the host -- though he or she may have planned everything down to the most meticulous detail -- neglected to take an assertive role in *bringing people together*. This doesn't necessarily mean that the host lacks social graces or has bad manners. It just means that a host who isn't taking a pro-active role in helping guests to meet one another has overlooked the single most important element in party planning.

Most of us envision a successful party as one where a room full of attractive, witty people laugh and mingle and eat and drink merrily, supported by good food, good liquor and good music. The room is packed with extremely interesting individuals, all of whom are quite capable of meeting each other, having stimulating conversations and keeping themselves amused and entertained. It has all the elements of a great party, right?

Don't be so fast to judge. Looks can be deceiving. If you look closely at the parties you've attended that fit this description, you might notice that while it appeared everybody was having a good time, the truth is they were probably straining to achieve this effect.

You've probably had the same experience yourself. After a while you got weary of struggling to meet people, of constantly going up to strangers and saying, "Hi. Are you a friend of the bride or the groom?" "Nice earrings." "What business are you in?" and other tiresome opening lines. And when the music is loud this exercise becomes truly pointless, because no one can hear a word you're saying and your throat starts to hurt from shouting. Your hosts haven't made much of an effort to introduce you to anyone, nor have they planned any kind of activity that would involve the whole group, which would help to break the ice and inspire people to interact. You probably left the party feeling unfulfilled because you never really managed to have a good conversation or learn anything about the other guests.

Learning to Host

From a host's point of view, things look completely different. As the host, the moment you make the decision to throw a party that your friends will rave about for years to come, you've committed to a task that will draw on your talents as circus ringleader, orchestra conductor and kindergarten teacher. It's a big responsibility with a lot of power, and it requires careful planning, political and psychological strategizing, and a limitless imagination.

People arrive at parties with high expectations, tempered only by their nervousness about meeting strangers. As the host, it's *your* job to make them feel secure and comfortable. Not unlike what a kindergarten teacher faces on the first day of school. Good parties require *leadership*, which is not a word one usually associates with an image of a lively party filled with people in a state of joyful abandon. But contrary to what many of us believe, leadership can make the difference between a great party and a dull one.

Once your guests start arriving, you're in charge of their comfort level. Whether things get off to a slow start (one or two early birds arrive 30 minutes ahead of everyone else) or kick right in at raging inferno level (50 people show up within 10 minutes), you need to be moving activities and people along as if you were choreographing a dance. Only in this case, the dancers don't know that they're being directed.

The reason games like "Pin the Tail on the Donkey" are played at children's birthday parties is because kids get bored just playing on their own. They need to be entertained and directed. Adults are a lot like kids in this way, only our play is different... we eat and drink, flirt and shmooze, but even that gets boring eventually, because we're usually working too hard at it. A good host can easily come to the rescue by engineering variations in the focus and energy level of the party. Party games and organized activities work like a charm and are always the best choice, but if you're not willing to go to that much trouble, then you can always depend on the most basic and primitive host trick in the book... working the room.

At my friend Ron's 50th birthday party -- a formal dinner at a country club where people were seated at round tables for eight -- Ron displayed the best example of working a room I've ever seen. Not only did he spend most of his time cruising from table to table greeting friends and thanking them for coming, but he also worked hard to find links between people and make sure this information was communicated.

At Ron's party my husband and I were seated at a table with three other couples. Round table seating is difficult because usually you can only speak comfortably with the people on either side of you, rather than trying to conduct a cross-conversation. We chatted casually with the people closest to us, until Ron showed up, and after some small talk, indicated the woman sitting directly across from me.

"Terri," Ron asked, "have you had a chance to meet Evelyn yet? You two have so much in common! She and her husband wrote a book together last year, they're both musicians, and they have a son the same age as yours."

With an introduction like that, of course I started talking immediately to Evelyn across the table, and since dinner was over and we were in the middle of dessert, it was acceptable for me to move over next to her to continue the conversation.

Ron did this at every table he visited, and would also bring people across the room to meet other people that he thought they'd be interested in. It was hosting at its finest, and Ron's efforts made the party comfortable and productive for everyone.

Ron's example is the ideal. This kind of expert networking doesn't necessarily have to be the exclusive domain of the host, but *somebody* should be taking responsibility for helping people make connections. You may not have an easygoing nature like π does, and if this is the case, you can try designating a friend with a dazzling personality to oversee this important aspect of your party. There's an enormous amount of work to do when you're the ringleader, and it helps to get as much support from friends as you can.

As the host, you should be present, available, awake and alive during your party, as opposed to overwhelmed and overworked. To attain this delicate balance, you need to use your energy where it will be most effective. You should <u>not</u> be spending your time:

- Cooking, serving or cleaning.

- Looking after children.

- Sitting quietly in a corner.

- Clinging to your spouse or date.

- Watching the game on TV in the den.

Instead, commit yourself to "working with your guests" as follows:

- Supervising things in the kitchen (but not working in there yourself if you can help it).

- Greeting guests at the door and showing them the way to the bar, the buffet, the pool, etc.

- Introducing people to one another (particularly those who appear to be having a hard time doing it themselves).

- Table hopping.

- Joining conversations in progress.

- Inviting others to join these conversations.

- Facilitating games, presentations and other activities.

Parties are like performances on a stage; showcases for introducing new faces, bringing new people into the fold, launching new relationships and building new families. But the simple act of saying hello to a stranger at a party sends many people into a paralyzing state of anxiety. What most people don't know is that *it's a host's responsibility to make it easy for people to meet and connect with each other.* After that, everything else is secondary. Planning great parties is an art that requires skill, experience and finesse. But even with a dazzling guest list, the finest food and a fabulously decorated home, guests can become uneasy as pressure to meet new people in an unfamiliar setting creates stress and anxiety.

This book was written because I've attended -- and I've heard about -- too many "bad" parties which could have been saved if the hosts had followed some simple guidelines about what makes parties work on an *emotional* level. In this book you'll find easy-to-follow suggestions and techniques for introducing people to one another, conversational strategies, activities that encourage interaction between strangers, and ideas for setting up situations in which guests have no choice but to meet and communicate. That, and that alone, is what parties are all about.

Parties can happen anywhere, any time for any reason, at homes, offices, restaurants or public parks. They can be casual back yard get-togethers with neighbors, children and dogs, or black tie affairs in hotel ballrooms. Powerful, important people go to children's birthday parties and family picnics just like the rest of us, so don't think you have to rent the Ritz to make your party a success. All you have to do is focus on the communication element of your party, and it will work like magic for everything from a formal wedding for 500 to a keg party in a parking lot. Remember that as a host, you have the ability to create a safe harbor for your guests, which is a feeling of comfort they'll always associate with you and your parties.

2. Party Games for Grownups

It rarely works to throw a group of strangers into a room together, give them some food, the latest wine-in-a-box and a little background music, and then expect them to fend for themselves. Although it would be nice if we could just assume that all party guests are good socializers, the truth is that most people aren't comfortable with strangers, and for the most part feel nervous and lost at parties.

A good host can make a big difference in the way a guest experiences a party by providing an activity *designed to encourage personal interaction*. It can be as quick and simple as gathering everyone together to sing happy birthday and watch the guest of honor open his gifts, or it can be an elaborate set-up like a murder mystery, which involves everyone throughout the entire party. Either way, a central focus, a humorous presentation or a group activity will harness the collective mind and produce these remarkable results:

- Individuals who have very little in common will be linked by a common purpose, if only for a few minutes.

- Strangers will be "given permission" to relate to one another during the activity.

- People can talk to each other about the activity after it's over.

- It will generate laughter and other emotional responses, which will help to loosen everyone up and provide a reason for future conversation.

Providing a central focus in a room full of people helps to unite everybody in common thought. It re-affirms their reasons for being there. It entertains them and warms them up, and helps develop their sense of belonging. As the host, you have the opportunity to inspire these feelings of comfort in your guests. But most hosts feel that it would be too aggressive and pushy to actually take charge and *manipulate people*, so instead, they opt to just leave their guests alone, and hope that everybody has a good time. Sometimes it works out fine, but it's more often just a matter of luck.

Children play games at parties because they have short attention spans and boundless energy that needs to be vented. They need to be guided and entertained to keep from becoming bored and cranky, and adults aren't much different. Working hard at meeting people and engaging in interesting conversations can get tiring after an hour or so. After you've made some small talk with a mildly interesting person or two, what do you do next? Where do you go? How do you find someone new to approach? Should you go into the back yard where the smokers are sitting? Maybe have another conversation with someone you met earlier? Have another drink? Go home?

This is when Party Boredom begins to set in. It's a common malaise brought about by lack of self-confidence, fear, need and stress. And once you've hit that low point, it's difficult to pull yourself out. This is the point where most people will choose to leave the party (and the host will wonder why everyone left so early!). But a good host can turn things around by taking charge and using some imagination. Here are some activities you can initiate, and the types of parties where they would be most appropriate:

Wedding Shower

My husband and I once hosted a wedding shower for our good friends Carol and Geoff. There were about 50 people in our home, a combination of his friends, her friends, and our friends, and most of them didn't know each other. We decided the party would work best if we organized a game which would bring us all together and help everyone get to know the happy couple a little bit better. The game we came up with was a home-version of the old TV show "The Newlywed Game." We had devised personalized questions for the Carol and Geoff, and the plan was to sequester one in another room while the other answered, just like on TV.

We began by announcing that we'd like everyone to gather in the living room. After taking a few minutes to explain how the game would work, we were up and running, and for the next hour, the entire group was laughing and participating. It was a riot, and everyone loved it. We videotaped the game, along with "interviews" with various friends who were present, and gave the tape to the bride and groom as memento of the party.

Casual Buffet For a Large Group

Rudy and Myrna are a couple who throw wonderful parties, where friends and family members (adults and kids) are all invited. The kids play outdoors or upstairs, and the adults gather downstairs to eat, drink... and sing! Rudy sets up his Karaoke system, which plays tapes of popular songs *without the lyrics*. The lyrics are displayed on video monitors (you can also have them simply typed on paper), and anyone who's so inclined can get up and belt out a favorite tune. Almost everyone participates, and those who don't, sing, laugh, dance and enjoy watching others perform. No one gives a hoot about being a "good" singer or performer. The atmosphere is casual, intimate and not the least bit pretentious. People stay until the wee hours because they're having too much fun to go home.

Intimate Dinner Party
for a Small Group

My friend Nancy Golden told me about this marvelous dinner-table game.

Guests are asked to bring a sample of a beloved piece of poetry, and throughout the courses of the meal, guests take turns reading their selections. It helps to have reasonably literate friends for this, but you can certainly substitute poetry with something else, like jokes, newspaper items, political quotes or even personal stories.

I did a variation of this last year with the people in my Spanish class. When our teacher went on vacation for several weeks, none of us wanted to give up our weekly study sessions, so I suggested that we have revolving pot-luck lunches which would take place every Wednesday at 11:30 am (the same time the classes had been held, so I knew everyone would be available). Each week, it was held at a different person's home, and all the guests would bring food and drink to share.

Because my son was in pre school at the time, I had access to beautiful bilingual children's story books from his school library. During lunch we'd pass a book around the table, each person taking a turn reading a passage in Spanish. The group (about 10 people) would then translate what was read. It was so much fun that we'd usually stay together for 3-4 hours doing this, and we were actually kind of disappointed when our teacher returned from Mexico and we had to give up our lunch parties and go back to school.

Baby Shower

At a baby shower given for my husband and me when our son was born, the hostess organized a game that provided us with beautiful memories to last our family forever. She called the room to order after lunch had been served, and passed out sheets of paper and pencils. Each guest had to write a little story about what kind of life they predicted my newborn son would have in 30 years, and then those who wished to could read their stories to the group. The results ran the gamut from poignant and sincere to hysterically funny, and included everything from a wilderness explorer who discovers an herbal cure for cancer in an Andean weed patch, to a corporate raider who wrests control of his father's business in a hostile takeover. I keep all these stories in a scrapbook, and can't wait until the day when we can all sit down and read them together twenty years from now.

New Year's Party

At some point during the evening, call the room to attention and ask volunteers to get up and say something about what the past year has meant for them. You'll be amazed at the stories and the responses you'll get. Someone might propose a toast to a friend who enjoyed a particular success during the year, pay a loving tribute to a wife, or announce a birth in the family. It's a great way to get up close and personal, and to reveal information to one another.

It helps to pre-select a few outgoing friends who will agree in advance to start things off. The host may want to be the first speaker, beginning by offering a toast to the many friends who came to celebrate, and congratulating specific individuals on personal milestones that occurred during the year.

After this presentation has concluded, your guests will know much more about each other, which will help link them together for further conversation.

Christmas Party

Janet hosts a Christmas party every year. She decorates her house beautifully, serves a lavish catered buffet, provides a full bar with bartender and invites everyone she knows, from the 22 year-old friends of her college-age children to retired older folks in her neighborhood and every kind of person you can imagine in-between. But the magic of Janet's Christmas party is the music. During the year, Janet sings in a high-energy, original-music gospel choir, and each year she hires the choir's director and a few of the members to perform at the party. Guests are invited to join in of course, and if you've never heard live gospel singing by talented singers who can wail and shout, you've really missed something. It gets the whole house shaking and jumping, and everybody dances and sings 'til their throats hurt.

Business Mixer

After the guests have been mingling for about an hour, call the room to attention and announce this simple ice-breaking game. Ask the group to form a circle and have each one tell a little about themselves and what their business interests are. Invite them to add personal information as well, like a few words about hobbies, families, recent accomplishments or personal goals. This is a common exercise for business-oriented gatherings where active networking is encouraged. And people enjoy being the center of attention for a few minutes. When the circle breaks, everyone will have chosen someone they want to meet based on what they've heard in the circle, and the conversation in the room will suddenly become more animated, more relaxed, and more productive.

General Games
That Work Anywhere

• Floating Board Games

In different areas of your house, set up a few different board games on various table tops, with little signs posted inviting people to play a game. It gives them something to do while they're standing around, and provides them with a way to connect with someone who happens to be standing nearby. Some game suggestions include Boggle, Scrabble, Pictionary or Trivia. Browse through a toy store and see what's available.

• Guess the Celebrity

As guests arrive, tape the name of a famous personality, live or deceased, to their backs. The name can be that of a film star, sports figure or literary personality, and might even fit with the party's theme. The rules are that each person a guest speaks to during the party can give them <u>one</u> hint about who "their" celebrity is. Yes or No answers are preferable. The one-hint limit sets it up so that the only way they can find the answer *is to keep talking to new people.* As each person figures out their mysterious name, have them report it to you. At some point later in the party (when the energy level needs picking up), make a little presentation in which you award prizes to the first two or three who guessed correctly.

• Large-Group Trivia

Near the front door, place a small basket with pencils and strips of paper, and a sign that says:

> "Write a trivia question about *(suggest some subjects like music, sports, geography, films, books, etc.)* and place your question in this basket. Later, we'll have a contest. If someone answers your question correctly, you both get a prize! Remember, you must know the answer to the question you submit."

Later on, call the room to order and read the questions out loud. Let the crowd shout out their answers, and then ask the question-writer to give the true one.

• Questions & Answers

This great ice-breaking idea comes from party expert Penny Warner, author of <u>Penny Warner's Party Book</u>:

After you've sent out your invitations and your guests begin calling to RSVP, ask each of them for a piece of news from their lives (a new job, a recent interesting vacation, a new baby in the family, etc.) Prepare a list of these tidbits, and when guests arrive at the party, give each of them a copy of the list. The object is for everyone to try to figure out which person belongs with which piece of news. For example, if the news is "he recently returned from a year in Europe," it's likely that during the evening someone who talks to the man in question will get this information from him. The point is to encourage people to share information and communicate *deeply* with one another about who they are, rather than just stand around making small talk.

• Theme Parties with Matching Games

I did a variation of the above-mentioned game for a party I gave to commemorate the 25th anniversary of the Woodstock music festival. As part of the overall theme, guests were asked to dress in hippie attire and bring along photos of themselves from the 60's (we defined the sixties as between 1965-1975). When people called to RSVP, I'd ask them to tell me a story about something of interest they did during this era, and I made a list of their stories. I then photocopied this list and handed copies to guests as they arrived. The object was for everyone to talk to each other during the party and try to find out which person matched which story.

At the same time, I also hung up a large sheet of butcher paper on the wall with a marking pen hanging from a string next to it and a sign that read: "please write down your 60's story." Later on, I read the stories to the group, and gave prizes for the best ones.

• Darts, Pinball, Video Games

It works in bars and pubs, why not in your home? You can rent pinball and video games, and have them stationed strategically around your house. It's a great ice breaker.

You'll notice that some of these games come with prizes. Prizes don't have to be dazzling or expensive, though in some situations it might be perfectly appropriate to give a good bottle of champagne or a silver business card case. But most prizes can simply be humorous and downright cheap. Lottery tickets (one dollar each!) make excellent prizes. So do those little humor books you find at bookstore check-out counters. Try coffee mugs, bags of homemade munchies, refrigerator magnets, kid's toys, old Louis Prima records from the 99-cent bin, and anything else you can imagine, from a pair of plastic pink lawn flamingoes (about 10 bucks) to a hand-made certificate of merit honoring the winner (free if you make it yourself).

At the Woodstock party, I gave out 3-D glasses that create rainbow prisms when you look at light through them. I'd purchased them earlier in the year at a fireworks show for a dollar each. They were a big hit, and matched the party's theme perfectly.

There are limitless ideas for simple networking games that are effective in encouraging people to mingle. For many hosts, however, the idea of speaking to a group and organizing that group into action is intimidating, but don't let that stop you. The solution is to find a friend who's got a funny, outgoing personality (everybody knows one), and ask him or her to help you out. You can even hire an emcee to keep things lively.

Try it next time and see what happens.

3. Business vs. Social Gatherings... Is There Really a Difference?

Miss Manners, in her book <u>Miss Manner's Guide for the Turn-of-the Millennium</u> offers this little tidbit:

"You do not use your own house or that of a friend to make business contacts, collect free advice, or publicize your achievements. Social occasions are for making romantic contacts, offering free advice to people not present, such as the President on what to do about the economy, and publicizing your children's achievements. You do not hand out business cards at social events.... you do not quiz other people, beyond the few pleasantries that help you pick a topic of conversation, on the subject of their occupations or employers, even if you are willing

to put in how 'how fascinating!' at regular intervals. Well-bred people go about socially for recreation, not to seek opportunities or to complain or brag about their jobs."

What??? Did I read this correctly?

If I weren't such a well-bred person myself, I'd tell Miss Manners what she could do with this little pearl of wisdom (and a some of her other ones as well). An attitude like this is not only unrealistic and archaic, but would make sense only for:

- Parents who do not work outside the home.

- People who have no life.

- Anyone involved in work which has no relevance whatsoever to society, the community, the economy or the world at large (I can't think of one job that fits this description, can you?)

- Old money socialites who can't identify with the concept of work, meaningful or otherwise.

I don't know with whom Miss Manners has been socializing, but I've written this book for intelligent people who are vibrant and alive, who have reasonable communication skills and some level of awareness of the world around them. For people who believe they are part of the whole human system, discussing the work they do is appropriate and relevant in <u>any</u> social setting.

And taking pride in one's work is one of the hallmarks of an emotionally healthy person.

By the time we become adults, hopefully we're involved in work that inspires some degree of personal satisfaction, contributes to the community, or at least provides a valuable perspective on the world. Does Miss Manners think that a woman with no children of her own who works as a nanny or a pediatrician has nothing to offer in a conversation about the achievements of someone's children? A nanny probably knows more about the local school system, child development, the latest toys for kids, and human psychology than most people. Because her contribution to the discussion is based on on-the-job observation, is it invalid or inappropriate? Of course not.

Another thing that hopefully happens to us when we become adults is that the work we do for money becomes less and less separate from who we are as people. Work is part of what creates our identities. Our work can be an expression of our personal affinities, our passions, and even our moral or ethical points of view. Our work environments are our communities, and they're as important as all the other communities we identify with (neighborhoods, ethnic groups, political alignments, family forms, gender). While not all people enjoy being defined by their job titles, most people, by the time they're 30 or 40 years old, have found a way to reconcile their work lives with their personal lives. Even the guy who drives the city trash truck has a view of the world that is indelibly linked to his role in it. In fact, he probably has a lot to say about recycling, the quality of life in the city, and local politics.

Work life is *not* separate from personal life, and an attempt to keep it separate results in a lot of lost people at a party struggling to find common ground. If you were having a birthday party for your child, and you wanted to introduce Johnny's mom, a recently divorced corporate attorney, to Tiffany's mom, a single mother who just graduated from law school, it would be irresponsible for you as the host to simply introduce them as "Johnny's mom" and "Tiffany's mom." You would be depriving them of valuable information that could lead to a stimulating conversation with the potential to launch an enduring friendship.

Regarding the handing out of business cards, almost everybody who works has a business card. It's a convenience. It saves having to search around for a pen with which to scrawl a phone number on the back of a soggy cocktail napkin. It's legible. It contains other vital information, like the name of your company, an address, a fax number or a pager number. This is the nineties, Miss Manners. Communication is everything.

To iron out the issue of proper behavior for business vs. social parties, think for a minute about the definition of sincerity. It means, in part, BEING THE SAME WAY WITH EVERYONE. If you are a confident person who's proud of yourself, your life, your family, your work or anything else you've created, then there's no need to wear one face for the business world and another face for the rest of the world. If you *are* living this kind of dual existence, the chances are you're pretty stressed out and unhappy, and you might want to consider changing a few things in your life. The highest and healthiest thing anyone can do is to be themselves, and parties are a good place to start.

Old Rules Of Behavior for Business Parties ... and How to Break Them

• Dress Like Everyone Else

One of the standards of 1950's corporate mentality was to honor conformity and to mistrust individuality. Forget that. Express yourself in your clothing. Have a personality. You don't have to be outrageous, just be an individual. Men, wear an artsy tie. Women, wear a flower in your hair. Develop a signature style, like wearing cowboy boots with your business suit.

• Don't Drink If Your Boss (Or Client) Doesn't Drink.

Unless of course you feel that drinking would cloud your ability to communicate. Or if the project you're working on is some kind of anti-alcohol campaign, in which case you shouldn't be working on it if you're a drinker.

• Don't Talk About Your Personal Life

Phooey. Let them know who you are. It's OK to tell them that you're going through a divorce, that your child is learning disabled or that you just ran a marathon. But don't give a lot of details (unless they're asked for), and don't cry on their shoulders about your troubles.

• Don't Bring A Date That Your Boss Or Client Wouldn't Approve Of

Whom you choose to love is none of their business, legally and ethically. However, if the issue isn't about lifestyle preference, but is more a matter of your partner being a sloppy drunk who always ends up with the lampshade on his head and routinely embarrasses you at parties, you might want to consider getting a new partner.

• Don't Express Your Personal Politics

If you're extremely passionate about your political ideals and your employer is so far over on the other side that it compromises your integrity, then you might want to get a different job. Or, you can make your position known, and be willing to deal with the consequences. There may not be any consequences beyond a stimulating debate, which would probably be great fun.

- ## Don't Indulge In Petty Office Gossip.

This is true. Don't do it.

4. Parties From Hell: Unforgettably Embarrassing Events

This book wouldn't be complete without a humorous look back at some of the worst parties in recent memory. Some of these stories are drawn from my own experiences, and others have been contributed by friends. The names have been changed to protect the innocent.

Lidia's Surprise Party for Robert

Early this year I received an invitation to a surprise birthday party for a close friend. The invitation was expensively designed, very formal, and requested my presence at an affluent country club for a glittery birthday bash. All this was being orchestrated by my friend's wife, and many of his important high-level business associates were also invited to mix it up with other interesting professional friends. It all looked very promising, until I noticed that party's vital statistics: guests were asked to arrive at 6:00 pm, on a *Friday* night, at a location that would require most of us to travel in bumper-to-bumper traffic during peak rush hour on the most congested freeway in the city.

The structure of this party forced the guests -- almost all of whom were working, professional people -- to leave their offices early in order to stop at home to change into formal party wear, *and to sit in crawling traffic for 45-60 minutes!*

I didn't arrive until 8:00, in the middle of dinner. My late arrival drew very little attention, and the hosts did not appear to be offended, since most everybody else also arrived late.

Rule:

Never start a party at 6 pm on a week night unless:

1. Your guest list includes only non-working people.

2. It's a business party or an office party.

3. It's a national holiday and everyone has the day off.

4. You live in a small rural town with no rush hour traffic and everyone leaves work at 5 pm.

Welcome to Washington...
Now Go Home.

John and Annie were two high powered New York lawyers, and when John was offered a prestigious position with an important government agency in Washington DC, they were thrilled, and looked forward to a bright future. The couple was even more excited when they received an invitation to a "Welcome to Washington" party thrown in their honor by a well known television journalist who planned to introduce John and Annie to Washington society.

They arrived at the party ready to be launched into their new glamorous life. They were greeted at the door by a maid, shown into a large formal living room where people were mingling, and were left there on their own. They didn't know one person in the room, and the famous TV journalist, whom they'd never met before, was nowhere to be found. Nobody greeted them, introduced them to other guests, or acknowledged them in any way, and as they made their way around the room feebly trying to introduce themselves to people, it appeared that nobody knew who they were, or that they were supposed to be the guests of honor. To this day, John and Annie still don't understand what happened. They enjoyed the party well enough, but never heard from the journalist or from anyone else who could explain the strange events.

Rules:

1. If you're going to tell someone that he'll be the guest of honor at your party, then treat him accordingly. That means you should make a special presentation to the group about him, or at the very least, make a point of introducing him to everyone and treating him as if he were someone important.

2. Always include a map or written directions to the party with the invitation. It's entirely possible that John and Annie had been given inaccurate directions, and showed up at the wrong house, where another party just happened to be in progress.

Jackson's Surprise Party for Amy

This surprise party was planned by the husband of the birthday girl. Both Jackson and Amy were extremely affluent, busy professionals, and I admired Jackson's ambition in trying to pull this off. However, he was not an experienced party-giver.

He began by inviting us all by phone, saying "show up any time after 8 pm." Most of us found this message on our answering machines, which required us to call him back for details and directions to the couple's new house, which none of their friends had yet seen. Return phone calls were to be made to Jackson's office, where he was usually unavailable, resulting in the need to leave a message with his secretary, which resulted in waiting for yet another call back from Jackson. In social circles where people are busy, this can mean as many as four or five phone messages exchanged before the directions to the party are ever given.

Jackson's "unique" idea for the surprise was that he and Amy would be having a quiet evening at home and then friends would start showing up at the door bearing gifts. Surprise! Fortunately for her, Amy's an easy-going person who isn't terribly attached to appearances, so she didn't mind that her friends arrived somewhat dressed up while she was wearing sweats and no make up. But I wouldn't advise trying this with most women. The good news was that the party ended up being pretty nice, with a small group of about 6 people engaged in stimulating and intimate conversation.

The bad news was that Amy and Jackson had not a stick of furniture in their new house, and we all sat on the floor. And the only food served, other than wine and birthday cake, was a bowl of fruit salad, which also sat on the floor in the middle of the circle of friends, next to a stack of bowls and some spoons.

Rules:

- A written invitation, complete with directions or a map to the party site is always preferred. This saves lots of time and phone calls.

- If you're a person who can't (or won't) prepare food, then get someone to help you. A bowl of fruit between six people is ridiculous.

- If at all possible, have furniture. Rent or borrow some if you have to. Lying around on the floor is fine if you're in your twenties and everybody's on drugs and listening to Jimi Hendrix. For people over 30, it can get very uncomfortable, even *with* the drugs.

Denise's 40th Birthday Bash

This very elaborate party was a black-tie affair held on someone's sprawling ranch, in a remodeled barn complete with a dance floor which had been installed for the occasion.

The party began at 7 pm, and everyone looked stunning in their gowns and tuxedos, cocktails in hand. The champagne poured freely, the hors d'oeuvres were wonderful, and the live dance band was hot. People ate, danced and mingled excitedly, and by all appearances, this promised to be a rollicking bash.

But as the hours wore on with the energy driving at a constant, boisterous high, something began to happen. People started to slow down, *and became bored.* At 9 pm, the buffet dinner was ready (it wasn't announced...people just started figuring it out and started drifting toward the buffet area). During dinner, the energy in the room remained at the same intense pitch. Some people ate while others danced, and the band continued playing loudly, making dinner conversation impossible.

Another hour passed this way with more of the same: return trips to the bar, a dance or two, maybe a new face to shout at over the loud amplified music. We had now been reveling freely for three hours, without the slightest alteration in the energy level, the sound level or any shift in the focus of our attention.

By 11 pm, everyone was either bored, tired or drunk. The plan was for the band to make a big birthday presentation at midnight, with a three-tiered cake, a cascade of balloons, a champagne toast and a special dance for the guest of honor and her husband. But by the time midnight arrived, we had been there *for five hours with no leadership,* and spirits were sagging.

Rules:

1. Always have an agenda. Take a leadership role and make sure events move along so that people are assisted in meeting one another and are given something to do .

2. Always shift the level of music, lights and energy according to new activities, such as dinner, gift-opening, presentations, etc.

3. Never let the music be so loud that people have to scream in order to be heard.

4. Announce to the room that dinner is ready, and in fact, announce any activity transitions. Take charge!

Mark and Adelle's Open House

This couple fancied the idea of an open house, and issued an invitation to their friends asking them to drop by "anytime between 2 and 6 on Sunday afternoon."

The problem: At any given time, only one or two people were present. Mark and Adelle would have the same conversation over and over again each time a new guest arrived (Louie's just gone into second grade, we're adding a room onto the house this Spring, our trip to Mexico was great). In some cases, this may be exactly what you want. But if you want a room full of people interacting and meeting one another, it's better to choose a specific time, so that they can all be there together.

Rules:

1. If you want to entertain more than one or two people at a time, and if you want your friends to meet one another, it helps to have them all in the room at the same time. An open house can sabotage this plan.

2. If you insist on having an open house, make it for a specific time (2:00 pm) rather than a range of time (drop by anytime between 2 and 6).

We're Having a Heat Wave... and You're Invited!

This was an outdoor party (with no pool) in late summer in 104-degree heat. The inside of the large, comfortable house had been deemed off-limits for some reason, and though the yard was set up with tables with umbrellas to provide shade, every one of the 25 guests was listless and miserable. We sat around panting like dogs, drenched in sweat. It was too hot to move around, so people found comfortable spots and stayed there, talking only with the people sitting close by. The umbrellas were no help.

Rules:

1. Don't plan mid-day outdoor parties in areas where summer heat can be unbearable and there's no shade.

2. Always have an alternative location or activity ready in case of unexpected weather.

Too Hip, Can't Talk

This 40th birthday party for a film industry executive was filled with interesting people, but they were difficult to talk to. Why? Because they were all in the same business and had worked with one another over the years. They knew industry secrets and shared personal gossip about mutual friends. As a result, conversations occurred in small, intimate groups and contained mostly shop talk about projects and co-workers. No effort was made on the part of the host to mix and introduce people (he was wrapped up in shop talk with close friends too). Only the most aggressive shmoozers (myself among them) had any luck engaging people in conversation, and we had to do this by boldly marching up to groups of people and assertively introducing ourselves.

Rules:

1. Don't invite too many people from the same profession or the same company. Or, invite only these people and make it strictly a business party. For a social occasion like a birthday, add people of different ages and varied lifestyles.

2. Either way, get in there and introduce people to one another! And plan some kind of activity that will help your guests to feel more connected to each other.

The Baby Shower Surprise

A friend recently took me to a baby shower for one of her clients. The invitation gave the name of the restaurant and the suburb where it was located, but included no street address, directions or map. We had to call the restaurant from my friend's car phone to find its exact location.

We arrived (late, because we'd gotten lost) to find our group seated at a long table on an outdoor patio where several other parties were also in progress. The conversation was lovely, though we could only speak with the people on either side of us, while the guest of honor, who was seated at the head of the table, only spoke to those on either side of *her.*

We ordered from the menu, had a nice meal, and after lunch, the mother-to-be opened her gifts, though those of us at the far end of the table could see very little and hear even less.

None of this was really all that bad, but the final blow -- which qualifies the party for an honorable mention in this book -- was the way that payment of the bill was handled. When the check came, it was handed to the woman who was our alleged "host." She studied it, took twenty dollars from her purse, placed it into the leather folder which housed the check, and handed the whole thing over to the woman next to her. The obviously surprised woman quickly figured out that we were each expected to pay our own way, and followed suit, tallying her total, placing her money inside the folder, and handing it down the line. The problem was that *none of the guests had been told in advance that we'd be paying for our own meals.* It was embarrassing for all, not to mention a financial hardship for some.

Rules:

1. An invitation to a party in a restaurant -- especially a baby shower or other significant event -- implies that the host will be paying the bill. If you're the host and you don't want to pay for an expensive group meal, then you can save a lot of confusion and embarrassment by having the party in your house (or someone else's). Make it a pot luck, or do the cooking yourself.

2. There's nothing wrong with having a dinner or luncheon party in a restaurant and asking your guests to pay their own way -- it's just like going out to dinner with a large group of friends. But if you're positioning yourself as a host (meaning you're throwing the party for a specific occasion or individual), then you have a responsibility to let people know in advance that this will be the arrangement. Tell them that it will be a dinner party with a group of friends, and that everyone will be paying their own way. You don't have to mince words. These are your friends, after all.

3. Always, without fail, include directions or a map to the party's location inside your invitation.

Tim's Annual Summer Party

This a is good example of a party that takes place in a beautiful setting but gets out of control because too many people are spread out in too many places.

Tim's house is a rambling 3-story, 8,000 square foot mansion with several side yards, a huge backyard, courtyards and other nooks and crannies. One year there were about 150 people there, moving from room to room in ones and twos looking for human connection. But because there were so many people and so many rooms in which they could get lost, it was difficult to do anything more than wander around aimlessly looking for a place to feel comfortable. Tim and his wife Marcy were rarely seen, as they too were wandering about. It was especially difficult for people who brought young children along (the invitation had said "children welcome"), because the frazzled parents spent all their time running around trying to keep their kids in sight. There was no agenda or event that would have caused everyone to be in the same room (or at least in adjacent rooms) at the same time, so everyone had to work hard at making contact.

Rules:

1. If your house is enormous, choose a specific section in which to hold your party and block off the rest of the place.

2. If you're going to invite people to bring their children, be sure you have a safe, manageable

place for them. If you don't, warn parents of this in advance, or provide child care.

These little stories touch on just about anything that can go wrong at a party within the realm of human communication. The good news is that these pitfalls and mistakes are easy to anticipate and easy to avoid. It just requires a little extra thinking about personal interaction. If your first priority is to make people feel comfortable and connected to each other, then the odds are good that you'll never go wrong.

5. Host and Guest Etiquette

Following is an interview with Syndi Seid, a marvelous woman who owns a unique business in San Francisco called "Advanced Etiquette." Syndi provides training and consulting in business and social etiquette and protocol throughout the world, and though many of her opinions differ from my own, her overall guidelines for host and guest etiquette are excellent. Here's a sample:

Q. *What is the primary responsibility of a good host?*

A As a host or hostess, it is your duty to handle every detail, from beginning to end, whether at home or in a restaurant. You should take time to organize the party in advance. Consider your guests' likes and dislikes. Anticipate his or her every wish. It is the host's job to watch over things; make introductions of people who may have common interests; and help stimulate conversations.

It is important to make people feel welcome in your home. If there is more than one host, one should stay near the front door to greet guests as they arrive and the other can help with introductions and other details.

Q.   Should a host plan games, presentations or other activities to keep guests entertained?

A   As adults it shouldn't be necessary to plan party games. As the host, do introduce guests, especially those you feel may have something in common. **As a guest, it is your duty to mingle and be gracious to the host and other guests.** Party games were planned when we were children to help overcome shyness. As grown-ups, it is your responsibility to mingle and introduce yourself throughout the party. There's a saying that guests should "sing for their supper."

Q.   Describe the best and worst parties you've attended

A.   The worst party was one where my husband and I were invited to dinner by a host who was a prominent psychologist at a major university, and a hostess who was a high-ranking doctor in a major hospital.

The hostess had taken extensive cooking courses in international cuisine, their beautiful home had been decorated by a leading interior designer. They had fine china and crystal and had coordinated solid sterling silver flatware. But the problem with this lovely setting was that neither one knew anything about how to host a successful dinner party. From the time we walked in the door until the time we left, the host and hostess did not take charge of various details.

They had a bar well stocked with bottles of scotch and other types of liquor, but they didn't think to furnish it with lemons, tonic water or other accompaniments to beverages. When it was time to be seated at the dining table, the hostess merely said, "oh, just sit anywhere." And as to the wine, the host asked for suggestions from the guests. The meal and overall surroundings were excellent, but the enjoyment of the entire evening was terribly stifled by the host and hostess not properly taking charge of things, mistaking what might be perceived to be a casual dinner party with appropriate behavior.

The best party was hosted by and old friend who recently had gotten married in a small wedding primarily for family. In order to introduce their friends to one another, to share their new home and to get acquainted in a more relaxed setting than a massive wedding, they decided to host one dinner party each month and invite eight friends to each party. The husband would invite four guests and the wife four. Before invitations were extended, both husband and wife would share and discuss their friends and create a guest list that would be fun and congenial. The invitations were extended and accepted by telephone with a reminder note sent a week before the dinner party, including directions to their home.

Upon arrival, the host greeted the guests at the door and coats were taken and hung in the hall closet. Hors d'oeuvres and champagne were passed by a server who was a student hired from the culinary academy. After about an hour of reception time, guests were invited to the dining room where the hostess directed each person to a chair and everyone was seated smoothly. The meal was simple and well planned. The courses were personally prepared ahead of time by both the host and hostess. The student server was hired specifically to serve the meal so the couple would not have to leave the table during or after each course.

At the conclusion of the dinner, the server cleared the table and everyone remained at it, enjoying cordials and talking until past midnight. Upon leaving, the host and hostess presented each guest with a small memento of the evening and of their marriage. It was the best small, intimate dinner party we had ever attended. Every detail was well thought out, and it made the evening enjoyable and memorable.

Q.   Should one always bring a gift for the host?

A   A rule of thumb followed in most cultures is that you should always bring a gift. It shows your appreciation for being invited. Although it is not required to write a thank-you note for basic party gifts, a thank-you note might be in order if you were presented with an exceptional, unique or extravagant item. As a guest, you should always write a thank-you note within 24 hours of the party.

Q.   It is rude to ask if you can bring a friend along?

A   It is definitely improper to bring an uninvited guest to a party of any kind *unannounced*. For intimate dinner parties it would be exceptionally rude where there may not be space at the table.

However, if your mother is visiting and staying with you, it would be acceptable to telephone and ask the host if you can bring her along. Especially if you know the party is a casual gathering with a buffet-style meal. Perhaps offer to bring an extra dish. No matter what, you should ask in such a way as to allow the host to respond and say it was not possible for whatever the reason.

Q.   What are the best ways to respond to introductions?

A.   In all situations, except the most casual backyard parties, it is best to either respond by saying, "Hello (first name and last name)" or to say "Hello Mr./Ms. (last name only)." Repeating the person's *full* name helps you to remember it and learn to say it properly. It is not usually appropriate to simply say "Hi." It should be reserved for the most casual settings among friends you have known for a long time.

Q.   How does one politely exit a conversation?

A.   No matter where or what the circumstances, it is rude to simply drift away from a conversation without saying a word. All you need to say is "Excuse me." However, if someone else drifts away from you, don't try to stop him or her to close the conversation. (*Author's comment: I prefer to say, "It's been wonderful talking to you. Good luck on your new business. I'm going to go mingle a bit now. I'll catch up with you later."*)

Q.   Is there a preferred way to greet persons with disabilities?

A.   If the person's right hand or arm is disabled, you would still extend your right hand and shake his/her left hand. It is improper to extend your left hand at any time for a handshake. When speaking with someone in a wheelchair, it is not necessary for you to lower yourself to be at his or her eye level. It's OK to look downward when conversing, but it's even better to stand back a few steps so the person seated doesn't have to stretch his or her neck to look straight up at you, and you won't seem like you're talking down to the person.

Q.   *What is the best way to deal with dinner party seating?*

A   Always defer to the host for seating instructions. Whether visiting an office or at a home, don't plop yourself down on the first chair you see. Wait to be directed to a chair, or ask "where shall we sit?"

Q.   *Is it impolite to move freely between rooms in someone's home?*

A   When visiting a person's home for the first time, do not go exploring without being invited to do so. Ask permission before going off and wandering throughout the house. Do not open doors where they are closed. And if you want to use the bathroom, ask the host to direct you, instead of finding it yourself.

This is also true for finding things in the kitchen. Only in the most casual situations among close friends would you ask the host permission to get something yourself. If you need some cream for your coffee, simply ask "Do you have any cream for the coffee?" To ask "May I have some cream?" implies that the host has some, and it may put him or her in an uneasy position to have to say " I don't have any."

Q.   Should guests ask the host if he or she needs help in the kitchen or with other preparations?

A   Don't ask to help in any way, except in the most casual settings among friends. Even among friends, whether at a formal or informal party, a guest should be the guest and allow the host to be the host. For a guest to help out, it compromises the situation and puts the affair into another dimension.

6. Holidays ... A Celebration of Life, Or a Family Anxiety Festival?

To many people (at least the ones who believe the Hallmark commercials) holidays evoke warm fuzzy images of loving families sharing a special day. It might be a snow-covered farmhouse at Christmas with smoke wafting from the chimney while adoring family members arrive to visit Grandma and Grandpa. Or a Thanksgiving table where a well-nourished American family says grace. We make sure that we have plenty of film on hand to capture those fleeting Kodak moments, and of course we keep the long-distance phone lines buzzing profitably with calls to out-of-town relatives. I once heard a statistic which reported that Americans spend $2 billion yearly on Christmas gifts and accompanying paraphernalia. Considering that there's such a lack of funding for education, health care and really important needs in this country, this made me so angry that I vowed to make charitable contributions in friends' names as gifts from that day forward.

Holidays *can* be loads of fun, especially the ones that warrant a day or two off during the work week. They're an excellent reason to have a party, even though the party's agenda may have nothing at all to do with the meaning of the holiday (how often does your family turn its Thanksgiving dinner conversation to the invasion of the Americas by the Europeans?).

In America, the major holidays come in two categories... religious (Christmas, Easter, Passover) and political (Labor Day, Memorial Day, Independence Day). We've all heard the adage that warns us against discussing either of these topics in mixed company, but for some reason on certain days of the year, millions of people get together to acknowledge events that may or may not speak to their personal religious or political beliefs.

But it doesn't matter. Because what these holidays really are to many of us is an excuse for a day off, and a good reason to visit with friends and family. Let's start with family.

It amazes me that major holidays like Thanksgiving and Christmas, and certain religious holidays like Passover, have a notion attached to them that they're "for family." Over the past few years I've taken on the responsibility of hosting Thanksgiving dinner at my house, inviting both family and friends. One year it happened that my husband's brother and his family was going to be out of town, so we accepted an invitation to Thanksgiving dinner at the home of a friend. A few days before the holiday, my brother-in-law called to say that his travel plans had suddenly changed, that he and his family would be in town after all, and that they'd decided to make dinner at their house. When we told him that in anticipation of his absence we'd accepted another invitation, he was enraged. "This is a family holiday," he fumed. "We should be together." And he actually asked us to cancel our other plans! He felt that he had priority because he was a relative, even though he'd not issued his invitation until the last minute and had already given us "permission" to go elsewhere by telling us he'd be away over the holiday. The outcome of this story was that my husband succumbed to his brother's pressure, and insisted that we adjust everything to accommodate said brother. We ended up going to both homes on opposite sides of town, one for dinner and one for dessert.

The point of all this is to illustrate the power of family politics when it comes to holidays. Along with food, gifts, a sense of community and a festive atmosphere, holiday get-togethers can be colored by expectations and pressure, guilt and family drama. And because most families are not of the Normal Rockwell variety, the drama often overshadows the festivity.

I've always found it odd to hear a grown adult say, "I'm going home for Christmas." She hasn't lived in that house for 20 years, and she has her own house and her own family. Does she really still think of her parents' house as "home?" It's interesting how when we're with our parents, especially if it's in the old family home, we're often made to feel like children. And once we're in the old homestead, we automatically start to operate from a need to seek parental approval.

Eric and Jack were two brothers who'd both moved to Los Angeles from New York when they were in their mid-twenties. Every year they went "home" for Christmas to visit their divorced parents... the mother in Long Island and the father in Manhattan. As the years went by, both brothers found wives, had children, and became successful in their careers. The first year that they traveled to New York with their wives and small babies to stay all together in their father's cramped Manhattan apartment, it became evident that this system was no longer manageable. The babies were cranky from the change in their sleeping schedules, there was no room for all these people in the apartment, and on top of that, the mother in Long Island wanted them to go back and forth between the two homes at least twice during their stay.

It was insane, but there was a history and a tradition there, and Eric and Jack refused to change the habit of going home for Christmas because "it would upset Mom and Dad." Eventually Eric was brave enough to show his parents the logic in changing this tradition by proposing this argument:

- The two brothers and their wives have to take time off from their jobs to make the trip each year. Conversely, the New York grandparents were retired and had plenty of time on their hands.

- Airfare for a family of four is expensive (kids pay full fare after 2 years old). The grandparents, who loved to travel anyway, could better afford trips to the west coast, wouldn't have to buy so many tickets, and could get senior citizen discounts.

- Traveling with small children is extremely stressful for everybody, and requires a lot of extra baggage for diapers, toys and other accessories. With all this stuff, plus four adults and three children, neither the apartment in New York or the Long Island house could accommodate the growing families.

The grandparents, to everybody's amazement, agreed to Eric's proposal, and from then on, the visits occurred in reverse. They now come to Los Angeles for holidays, usually on their way to some other exotic vacation or another, and enjoy the travel immensely. They can visit the kids and the grandkids in comfort, and don't have to do all the extra cooking and housework that was once part of the yearly ritual.

Imagine what the holidays would have been like if Eric hadn't dared to question family tradition.

Creating Your Own Holiday Rituals

As liberated adults, with or without children, you can create your own holiday traditions, make up your own rituals, and even invent your own religious faith.

I personally find it difficult to abide by certain traditions because of my disdain for organized religion. So when I became a mother and realized that I'd have to explain these religious holidays to my son, I did some research and found out what many of the original meanings were. I learned that Christmas was originally a celebration of the Winter Solstice. Jesus was born in the Spring. Christians simply superimposed his "birthday" on the solstice celebration to make it convenient, to merge some of the symbols, and to give the people something joyful to do in the dead of winter. The solstice symbols include an evergreen tree, which represents the ability to survive through winter. Other typical Christmas scenes, like the cozy snow-covered cottage with the fire burning in the fireplace and warm cookies on the table, are symbols of comfort, warmth and survival through the cold months. Getting together with friends and family for a feast is also about winter survival in the community. St. Nicklaus was actually a guy who lived in about 300 AD who freed enslaved children as part of a political movement. Thus his giving of "gifts" to little ones.

The same is true for Easter, which was originally, in the pre-Christian period, a fertility celebration addressing the rebirth of plant and animal life, and the beginning of the planting season. Thus the bunnies and eggs, which symbolize reproduction, and the flowers and pastel colors which are indicative of Spring.

From this amalgam of information I created my own system of beliefs and symbols. It works for me, because my personal definition of God has more to do with nature and life cycles than fear, rigidity and moral judgment. At my son's school, the teachers and children put on a "Spring" show and a "Winter" show. They don't call it Christmas and Easter because the school's demographic make up is so ethnically diverse that they don't want to offend or exclude anyone. So even though in the Winter show they have Santa Claus and the kids sing Jingle Bells, they also have selected children and their families come up to the stage to make presentations about their own cultural links to the season. A Chinese girl and her mother tell the audience about Chinese New Year. A Jewish girl and her father make a presentation about Chanukah. And last year, my son and I got on stage and talked about Solstice, which has now become our family's holiday. We have friends and family over for dinner, and we have our "solstice tree" decorated with stars, bells, ribbons, beads, ornaments, popcorn strands... all the usual stuff. There's a wreath on the front door made of pine and winter berries, and of course, we exchange gifts.

Certainly traditional celebrations are wonderful, egg nog and all that for Christmas, a picnic in the park on Labor Day, and fireworks on the Fourth of July. If you're going to have a party, just use the guidelines for any party to make it a success. But if you're looking for something different to try, here are a few ideas for celebrating traditional holidays in less-than-traditional ways, which might help to make the holidays a little more meaningful for you:

Christmas

- If Solstice isn't your cup of tea, use Christmas as an opportunity to really love your neighbors by inviting them to dinner. Invite friends or co-workers who you know will be alone on Christmas, even if you've never socialized with them before. Or call your local social services agency to find out about any volunteer work you can do during the holiday season.

- Instead of combing the malls for obligatory gifts that the recipients probably won't use anyway, make contributions to your favorite charity in the names of your friends. Send each friend a card that says "In the spirit of the season, we have made a contribution to Childhelp USA in your name ." And include a flyer or pamphlet about the organization with the card.

- Go to a warehouse club store and purchase large quantities of staple foods (rice, beans, pasta, canned goods) and other items (toilet paper, toothpaste, toys, clothing) and take them to a homeless shelter, women's shelter or local office of your favorite charity. Have a picture taken of yourself doing this (in front of your car loaded up with the goods), and make it into your photo

Christmas card. Send it to your friends to let them know what you did for Christmas, and invite them to join you next year (thanks to Mary and David for this idea).

- Organize a group of friends to go caroling at hospitals, retirement homes or homeless shelters on Christmas eve.

Thanksgiving

- Instead of a huge dinner with family and friends, volunteer to be a food-server at your local homeless shelter or mission.

- Acknowledge the Native Americans, who are the real heroes of the Thanksgiving story, by getting some books of Indian poetry or ritual from the library, and having your guests take turns reading interesting selections from them during your meal.

- Take a vacation and visit an Indian reservation to see what really happened after the pilgrims arrived.

Passover

- This holiday acknowledges the freeing of the Hebrew slaves from Egypt, who were led by Moses out of bondage after an intense negotiating session with Pharaoh. If you would like to make Passover a bit more relevant to modern concerns, try adding some text of your own to the Passover seder, which would include the acknowledgment of all slaves everywhere in the world, throughout history. You can mention the slavery that still exists today, and when you get to the part about the plagues, add some of our contemporary plagues, like AIDS and world hunger.

- Invite someone from another culture or another religion to share in the seder with you.

Easter

- Invite some kids over for an egg hunt in your yard. Let them plant a few seeds in your garden in honor of Spring.

- Have your Easter dinner outdoors.

- Put a May pole up in front of your house (an ancient symbol of Spring).

New Year's Eve

- For a change of pace, have your party on New Year's Day. It's more cost effective and safer than going out and paying an inflated price for dinner on New Year's Eve, and then driving home on the road with a bunch of drunks.

- Stay home and invite a few friends in for a quiet New Year's dinner. Rent a movie, play a game, or watch some of the New Year's Eve TV specials.

- Stay home with your significant other, build a fire, drink champagne and make love in front of the fireplace at midnight.

Memorial Day

- Go on a peace march or visit veterans in hospitals.

- Go see the AIDS quilt .

- Volunteer for an organization that works for world peace.

- Make a home video of someone in your family who has experienced war first-hand. Let him talk about what it was like, complete with reminiscences about friends who were there, horror stories, funny stories and anything else he wants to say (veterans need to do this). This tape can become a valuable family treasure, and a profound reminder to us all.

Coping With It All

Using creative alternatives and designing your own rituals can ease a lot of the stress and depression that often accompanies holidays. If you're deeply enmeshed with family and friends, or you've been cooking, cleaning and working for days on end, remember to take some time out for yourself. You'll feel better if you can regenerate a bit and keep yourself relatively healthy. It *is* possible to take care of yourself emotionally and physically during the holiday party season. Here are some suggestions:

- Try to eat well. Instead of having a second piece of pumpkin pie, leave the table and go play with the kids, or invite grandma to take a walk with you.

- Drink lots of water to keep your system clean while you're filling it with sugar, alcohol and fat.

- Lighten your load. If you're cooking Thanksgiving dinner for 18 people, get help. If you can't, then make sure you rest when you can. Take a nap.

Put a chair or stool in the kitchen so you can get off your feet occasionally. Ask friends or family members to help out by bringing side dishes, desserts or other items. Hire a baby-sitter to watch the kids.

- Don't go off your exercise regimen. Even if you're traveling to visit friends or family, try to at least take a walk every day.

- Consider doing something completely different next year, like a ski trip or a vacation in the Caribbean.

7. Parties for Children... Honoring the Short Attention Span

If there's one thing everyone needs to remember about kids parties, it's this: kids create chaos. <u>Don't add to it.</u>

One Sunday afternoon a group of seven year-olds and a few of their parents gathered for Janie's birthday at a mega video arcade and miniature golf course. There were several parties going on simultaneously, each under a decorated canopy, while about 500 other people spread out around the vast acreage, playing kiddie golf outside and video games inside. Pizza was served, followed by birthday cake and a round of miniature golf, finally winding it all up with a few games in the arcade.

Sounds like a fine idea for a party. But the place was huge, and the children were energetic and difficult to keep contained (there were about 20 kids and 6 adults). The host's solution was to assign each of the adults a group of kids to supervise, which meant taking the kids through the golf course, making sure they didn't get lost, and seeing to their bathroom needs. It seemed like fun at first, at least for the parents who were assigned mild-mannered kids. But for those of us who'd come to the party expecting to sit idly chatting with other parents while the kids entertained themselves, the idea of suddenly being responsible for a group of 7 year-olds on a sugar high was more than we'd bargained for. By the time everyone got to the video arcade, with its hellish noise and high anxiety level, the parents were frayed around the edges and at the end of their patience. It was not a pretty sight.

Kids love activity-oriented parties, but parties held in large public spaces have their own unique set of problems, not the least of which is the need to protect the children *from the public*. In big cities (and everywhere else), it's not advisable to allow a child to go to a public restroom alone. It depends on the child and the location of course, but some experts say that children under 12 should always be accompanied by an adult (or at least have an adult waiting outside the restroom door). Very young kids need adult eyes on them constantly, so managing a birthday party for a group of 5 year-olds in a crowded park can really be a headache unless *each* child is accompanied by an adult.

If you really have your heart set on bringing a group of kids under age 10 out in public, try to select an easy-to-supervise, *contained space* for them. The first time I went along as a volunteer parent on a field trip with my son's pre-school, I learned that it's easier to watch a group of kids by visually patrolling the perimeter of a given space; keeping an eye out for strays rather than trying to keep track of each individual little body as it runs and plays (ask any sheep dog). The key here is that there has to be a perimeter, like a clearly marked picnic area in a park, a balloon-lined lane for a bowling party, or a special section set aside for your group at the local fast food restaurant.

But even these settings have their risks if you've got more than three or four kids. If you're planning to depend on other parents to oversee the well-being and safety of kids in a large group, be sure there are no more than 3 kids per adult. It's a good idea to let the parents know in advance that they'll be expected to pitch in, and give them a chance to decline the invitation if they wish.

Overall, the best party for kids is one in which they can have a lot of freedom without being in danger. The best way to do this is to either have the party in a visually manageable space like your backyard or house, or invite only a few special small friends. The ideal party for a seven year old might be to take her and her best friend to Disneyland. One mother took her 8 year old son and his three best buddies on a Tuesday night to Johnny Rockets -- a 50's style diner with an "American Graffiti" decor and loud music -- and let them sit in their own booth while she sat in another (still able to see them of course). The boys had a ball, and it was special because they got to stay up late on a school night. At eight years old, they're better at focusing on one or two friends than relating to a group anyway, so why not tailor the event to the child's comfort level and social abilities?

For younger kids, organized parties at your local "Kids Gym" are a good bet. Check the listings in your regional family magazines or ask friends about how to find these places. Kids as young as six months old can play freely in a large, safe room filled with equipment for climbing, crawling, touching, running, throwing, rolling, and everything else kids love. And, for the price of the party, you also get the services of the trained staff who supervise and play with the children. Kids over three can be dropped off and picked up when the party's over.

If you have a party in your home, make sure the house and yard are safe and clean. I remember going to a backyard party for a one year-old where the little guests were crawling, lying, sitting and otherwise hanging around on the grass The host family had two giant dogs, and the grass was yellow and dead in selected spots from years of accumulated droppings. At one point, I witnessed one of the dogs squat and urinate about two inches from a crawling baby. It was a real turn off.

Remember... kids create their own chaos. But you can keep the chaos under control by enlisting others to help you manage the party. Hire older kids, like your babysitter, a teen age girl from the neighborhood or an older sibling to help with "kid wrangling," minor kitchen chores or after-party clean-up (they're affordable, and perfectly capable of these tasks). Or ask friends, grandparents or elderly neighbors to chip in.

Children and Food

For kids, eating junk food is part of the party spirit, but there's no reason to poison the little guys. If you're going to serve cake, ice cream and lemonade, then you've already included all the sugar and fat a human body can stand for one day. You don't need to add M&Ms, lollipops, cookies or potato chips. Try to balance it with carrot sticks, olives, finger sandwiches of peanut butter & jelly, crackers & cheese, or fruit. If you're planning to give out party favor bags, fill them with little toys, not candy. The same is true for piñatas (pack them with toys instead of sweets). Your kids will feel better for it.

Children and Gifts

All kids eventually figure out that the main point of a birthday party is to collect gifts. One way to remove some of the importance from presents is to break tradition and put off opening them until the party's over. The old style party where a gleeful kid opens one brightly wrapped box after another and proudly displays the booty to a room full of admiring (jealous?) peers seems to be less and less popular each year (at least in my neighborhood). Very young kids get bored and can't really concentrate on the spectacle, though older kids enjoy oohing and aaahing over the cool new stuff. But there's always the potential for a riot breaking out when they all want to play with the new toys and the birthday girl doesn't want to share. Better to wait until all the guests have gone home, and then open presents with just the family gathered around. It makes a lot more sense, and adheres beautifully to the rule about not adding chaos.

And by the way, don't forget to help your child write and send thank-you notes when it's all over.

12 Helpful Hints for Having a Kid's Party

by Penny Warner
author of
KIDS' PARTY GAMES & ACTIVITIES:
Hundreds of Exciting Things to Do at Parties

1. Select a theme. A favorite toy, special movie or often-watched TV show makes a good theme, complete with food, favors, decorations and fun to match.

2. Think the party through. Plan your time -- two hours in the afternoon is best -- and try to imagine the time allotted for the welcome, games, activities, presents, cake and good-byes.

3. Invite your child's good friends and keep the group manageable. You don't have to invite everyone your child has ever met. Too many kids overwhelm everyone.

4. Hire a baby sitter to help during the party if you can't round up adult volunteers. Helpers will be invaluable during game time and can watch the kids while you prepare food.

5. Plan to have both quiet and active games to balance the kids' energy levels. Start with a quiet game, offer one or two active games, then wind up with another quiet game.

6. Over-plan the games. A party can turn to chaos if there aren't enough games and activities planned, so be sure to have a few alternatives if the games run short.

7. Tie the games and activities to the party theme by re-naming the games or using props to complement the theme.

8. Have prizes for both winners and losers, and don't place too much emphasis on winning to avoid disappointments.

9. Keep the sweets to a minimum and provide some healthy snacks so the kids don't get too strung out on sugar.

10. Keep the cameras handy -- both video and still cameras -- so you'll have a record of the fun.

11. Buy a copy of *Kids' Party Games and Activities*.

12. Buy a copy of *Kids' Holiday Fun* to help you plan something special with your kids every month of the year.

Excerpted with permission from
KIDS' PARTY GAMES & ACTIVITIES:
Hundreds of Exciting Things to Do at Parties
by Penny Warner
- Meadowbrook Press -

8. Common Party Problems

There are several basic glitches that have the potential to do serious damage to an otherwise great party. These problems are universal. They can occur anywhere, at any event. But the good news is that every one them can be either avoided or addressed with success. Here are the leading contenders:

• People Show Up Late

There is absolutely nothing you can do about this other than to make them feel guilty, stop inviting them to future parties, or speak to them about it directly. For dinner parties, when showing up on time is imperative because serving the meal is timed precisely, it's just plain rude for guests to arrive late (at least not without a great excuse). I generally refuse to delay a meal because we're waiting for a late guest who hasn't bothered to call and give us permission to start without him. Which is more rude?

That he shows up to find everybody eating without him, or that he didn't call to let us know he'd be late? It's your judgment call of course, but if you want to keep 8 hungry people waiting for a dinner that's going to be dry and overcooked because Paul lost track of the time at the office, then feel free.

If you have friends who are chronically late, the obvious solution is to give them an earlier arrival time that the other guests. If you want to serve dinner at 8:00, tell this particular friend that dinner will be at 7:30 or even 7:00, depending on the seriousness of his or her   lateness habit.

Occasionally lateness is quite excusable. For example, as a parent, I've learned that with very young children in the house it's often impossible to get somewhere at a particular time. Many times we've been invited as a family to a 4 pm barbecue, only to find that our toddler didn't fall asleep for his much-needed nap until 3, and we didn't want to wake him prematurely because he's just getting over a fever and he needed the rest. Not to mention the fact that if woken, he'd be cranky, overtired and miserable, and terrible company at the barbecue. However, I would *never* neglect to call the host to explain the situation, and I would certainly not expect her to hold dinner up for us.

• Men and Women Break Into Separate Groups

There is a formula which almost always results in men and women spending the evening in isolated groups divided along gender lines. In a nutshell, here's how it tends to happen:

1. Most of the guests are married couples, usually over age 50.

2. Most of the couples already know each other well.

3. There is no central activity planned for the group as a whole.

A good example can be found in the social life of my parents, who live in a retirement community where they've formed close friendships with an intimate group of like-minded folks. Most of the people in the group are married couples who see each other often, and when they get together at someone's home for a dinner, birthday or holiday party, the room inevitably splits in half; the men in one area and the women in another. Not unlike the way it was when we were thirteen years old and attending our first school dance (do you suppose we revert back to this as we age?).

People do gravitate toward their own gender when they're not looking for a romantic encounter. Also, among retired couples, the men and women have probably already spent the whole day at home together getting on each others nerves, and they need a break. I'd venture to say that in my parents' generation, women probably expect male conversation to be boring, focused on their medical problems or political views (which the wives have been listening to for years), and the men probably believe that women's talk is boring too, centered on gossip and grandchildren. I haven't observed this in younger people, so I suppose the generation gap might account for much of it. Though in parts of the culture where work and interests are still divided along traditional gender lines, this kind of separation must certainly occur (men talk about sports and cars; women talk about children and recipes).

If this happens at your parties, there are a few simple things you can do. Most importantly, be sure you've planned a focus or activity that can involve everyone (see Party Games). Asking men to help in the kitchen (where the women are likely to be clustered) is another way to mix up the sexes. If you're comfortable taking charge and you have a sense of humor, request that people sit with other people's spouses because you're tired of having a girls section and a boys section. It also helps to design the party so that it takes place in more than one room, which encourages people to move around.

And work to bring people in and out of each other's conversations! For example, if five men are standing around talking about politics, you, a woman, should join in, and as the conversation heats up, invite another woman in the room to join the group in discussing this fascinating topic. You're the host, and it's your job to keep things moving and mixing.

• People Don't Mix With One Another

Throughout this book, you'll see many reasons given for why people, left to their own devices, don't mix well. But if there's one thing to remember, it's this: *as a host, you are required to actively bring people together.* It's your most important function. If you feel that you'd be intruding on someone's privacy if you brought someone interesting over to meet him, the chances are you're wrong, and it would be worth your while to take that chance. If it turns out that your friend is offended by your having done this, then he has no business being at the party.

Most of us are taught as children that it's impolite to "force" ourselves on other people. Traditional etiquette tells us that it's better to be quiet and unassuming than to draw attention to ourselves. If we followed this line of reasoning, we'd never speak to other people! And sadly, a lot of people, whether they know it or not, really do operate this way. As a host, it's your responsibility to literally move people around into new and interesting conversational groups, and to provide as many introductions as possible.

• People Don't RSVP

I've been told that this isn't much of a problem in some circles. But it's happened to me over and over again. How to do you make them call? Once, as a joke, my husband and I printed on a party invitation: "A

$5,000 reward will be paid to the first three people who RSVP." We didn't mean it of course, but some people didn't call until the day of the party and still asked for the five grand!

There's not much you can do about this other than printing very clearly and loudly on the invitation: "*PLEASE* RSVP." Or you can include a little message, such as "we would very much appreciate an RSVP no later than December 4th." Some people ask that guests RSVP "regrets only," which saves a lot of phone calls and head-counting.

• People Won't Leave

It's 1:45 am. Your going-away party was a smashing success, so much so that 6 guests are still sitting in your living room putting the finishing touches on their debate on health care reform. Or at least, you *hope* it's the finishing touches. You're exhausted and long to be in your bed, and you have to get up early tomorrow to run last-minute errands and pack for your 2-month excursion up the Amazon. But this last group of die-hards show no sign of winding down. What do you do?

Tell the truth. Sit down in the middle of their group and simply say, "you guys, I love you to pieces, and I'm so glad you came, but I've got to go to bed now. You're welcome to stay if you like, just remember to lock the door behind you when you leave."

If you're uncomfortable being that direct, or if you really don't want them to stay after you retire, start cleaning up the house, putting things away, taking the extra chairs back out to the garage, and turning off lights. That will give them the hint.

• People Bring Friends Without Asking You First

Once they're at your front door, there's not much you can do about it. However, if your friends have manners, they'll call first and ask if it's OK to bring someone along. Ninety percent of the time adding more people makes for a better party, so go with the flow and have an attitude of "the more the merrier." However, if there's a specific problem, such as lack of space or a meal that's been pre-paid for a certain number of people, you have no choice but to say so.

This reminds me of the story about the mysterious stranger, which has no point really, but fits perfectly here.

I once threw a party for 30 people at an intimate restaurant, and a strange man showed up. He said he was a friend of John and Sabrina, who couldn't make it, and that they'd asked him to attend *in their place.* Nobody knew him. He hardly spoke to a soul all night, and he was a very weird guy. We tried to act gracious, figuring John and Sabrina had a reason for sending him, though they'd never asked us if they could send a "representative." When we next saw John and told him about this, he said he hadn't a clue who this person might have been, and claimed to have no recollection of having told anyone about the party. So I showed John the photos we took that night, and pointed out the mysterious stranger. John said, "Oh, that's my neighbor George. What on earth was he doing there? How would he have known about your party?"

My guess is that John *had* mentioned the party to George, however casually, and told him that he and Sabrina wouldn't be there. Or maybe George found the invitation in John and Sabrina's trash can. George, being a lonely guy (with a lot of guts) decided he would just show up. I kind of admire him for this.

Anyway, the point is, don't add your friends to someone else's party mix without permission. It might be the last invitation you ever receive from them.

• Neighbors Complain or Call the Police

This situation can and should be avoided. The solution is to inform your neighbors well in advance that you'll be having a party with a live band in the back yard (in writing, on a flyer distributed by you to their mailboxes). And consider inviting them! But there's always the chance that the curmudgeon in the house behind yours who complains about everything will stay true to form when it comes to your party, so be considerate of him and everyone else on your block. Keep the music at a manageable sound level. And have the band finish at 11 pm sharp. After that, move the party into the house and listen to recorded music.

If your neighbors call the police because your guests are rowdy, drunk, driving recklessly on the street, shouting obscenities on the sidewalk and urinating on their lawns, then the neighbors are doing the right thing, and you're not.

• Not Enough Parking on Your Street

This is often a problem. and there are several ways to address it:

1. Hire a valet parking service (check the yellow pages).

2. Ask people to car pool

3. Be sure to mention your parking problem <u>on the invitation,</u> and offer alternative parking sites (with a map).

4. Hire or recruit someone with a van to shuttle people from an alternative parking site to your house. Keep in mind that this service will need to be available for the duration of the party.

Drunk, Violent or Unruly Guests

Believe it or not, there are pockets in our culture where it is recommended that arriving guests be searched for weapons or dangerous drugs before being allowed in. I don't suppose many of those people bought this book, but for those times when you might have to deal with a guest's behavioral problems, here are few ideas:

• Someone is Overly Intoxicated on Drugs or Alcohol

There are several different ways this scenario can go, but first and foremost, don't let him drive! Make arrangements for a friend or a cab to take him home.

If the person isn't really bothering anyone but is dysfunctional, making a fool of himself or embarrassing other guests, try to send him home (in a taxi or with a sober friend). If he won't go, offer him a place to lie down, just to keep him away from everybody else. As the host, you can be held legally liable for damage or injury that occurs because of this person, so act carefully. If the person is so seriously affected by the alcohol or drugs he's ingested that you feel he might be in physical danger, don't hesitate to call 911.

• A Serious Argument or Confrontation Breaks Out at Your Party

It can be a marital spat that suddenly breaks out between a couple, or two macho guys fighting over the fact that one tried to hit on the other's girlfriend. It can even be a political argument that heats up a little too much. If it looks serious, by all means, intervene by asking them to either take it outside or leave. Don't get involved, and don't try to help settle it. Your responsibility is to take care of your party. Not to fix your friends' lives.

• A Guest Acts Obnoxious and Irritates Other Guests

If you're receiving complaints or overhearing comments about a particular guest behaving offensively, you may have to remedy the situation. For example, Joe may going around telling racist jokes which are making people extremely uncomfortable. Or overly-hormonal Jason, after a few drinks, is coming on with crude sexual innuendoes to every woman in the room.

If someone brings this to your attention (especially if it comes from more than one person), quietly take the offending guest aside and let him know, in a supportive way, that his behavior is causing problems, and that he might want to tone it down because he's embarrassing himself. Don't hesitate to enlist the help of friends in this effort if you need it.

9. Wedding Wisdom

A couple of years ago when I worked as the travel editor for a bridal magazine, I came across a term called "bridal tyranny." I fell in love with this expression because it had been a year in which I'd been a bridesmaid in four different weddings. I disliked most of these experiences immensely, and after each wedding, I vowed never to do it again. In fact, on the way home from one of them, I removed the dyed satin pumps (a lovely shade of peach) which had been killing my feet all night, and hurled them out the car window. They landed on someone's lawn.

Bridal tyranny. It's a temporary condition that strikes the majority of brides regardless of their chronological age or the emotional maturity they might display in other areas of their lives. It's more common in younger brides than older ones, though I've seen 40-year olds who are otherwise easy-going transform into control freaks when it comes to planning their weddings. At the risk of sounding sexist, this doesn't seem to happen to men. I haven't heard many stories of bridegrooms getting hysterical over shoe-dye colors or insisting that members of the wedding party wear the exact same shade of misty lilac panty hose.

Giving Up Control

Weddings are uniquely personal events. It's a way for a couple to make a statement to their community about their commitment to each other. For guests, it's an opportunity to share in the couple's happiness while being touched and entertained by the spectacle of the ceremony. But the preparation leading up to the big day can be unbearably stressful because of the intense long-term planning. For some reason, people who are otherwise reasonably sane and can deal with reality in normal life suddenly feel the need to insist that everything be perfectly flawless for one day. This is absurd. My primary recommendation when it comes to planning weddings: let go of the quest for perfection. It doesn't matter, and you'll never achieve it anyway. Ask any therapist.

Here are some examples.

At the wedding of my husband's father Ed to his second wife Barbara, some uncontrollable turn of events caused the caterers to forget to show up. The ceremony began on schedule even though there were no tables and chairs and no food to be seen. After the ceremony was over, they ended up sending out for pizza to feed 75 people. Some would consider this a disaster. Ed and Barbara consider it one of the sweetest, most treasured stories of their life together.

At my own wedding in 1987, which was held in the back yard of my brother-in-law's house, it began to rain lightly in the middle of the ceremony. My husband and I laughed with joy at the cosmic beauty of this occurrence, and about 90 percent of the guests who were seated under the stars felt the same way. A few ran for cover, but most held their ground, so enchanted were they by the whole thing. The caterers had to move their operation indoors, and it was quite a crush inside the small living room of the house. Did we care? Did anyone? Not a bit.

What happens during your own wedding is that you get so caught up in the moment that all the planning, all the minuscule details that mattered so much only yesterday suddenly mean absolutely nothing. A rabbi once told me that couples go unconscious during their wedding ceremonies. It's a combination of stage fright and emotional overwhelm. Suddenly you don't care what kind color shoes the bridesmaids are wearing. And then, as a new bride once told me, "the next thing you know, you're lying on a beach in the Bahamas and the whole thing is over."

The kind of control many people attempt to exert over nature, other people, the natural flow of things and life in general reaches obsessive proportions when it comes to weddings. At the wedding of Wendy and Harold for example, the bride insisted that each bridesmaid (myself among them) wear an identical pair of tiny pearl stud earrings. To insure our compliance, she even bought them for us, giving them to us as gifts at her bridal shower. The dresses she chose for us were of a stomach-churning pale orange hue, she insisted that we wear the exact same color stockings, and as tradition dictates, we were required to buy little satin shoes and have them dyed to match. We were also, of course, expected to pay for the dresses, shoes and stockings ourselves ($250) and to wear them happily, even though one of the bridesmaids was seven months pregnant and was miserable in high-heeled pumps. And I was allergic to the posts of most pierced earrings (even real gold, which these were not).

I didn't wear the prescribed earrings, and Wendy is still angry at me for this. When a few months later I was asked to be a bridesmaid at my friend Jane's wedding, and she showed me sketches of the slinky form-fitting dresses she wanted to have custom made for her attendants, I spoke up. "Please don't do this Jane," I said. "You may be five-foot-nine and have a body like a model, but the rest of us don't, and we'd look terrible in these dresses." I also reminded her that each woman in the wedding party was well over 30 years old, and we were *individuals,* with individual identities that we'd carefully developed over the years. Why try to make us look all the same? A color-coordinated flock of virginal maidens dressed up like pastel flowers all in a row may work for a 22 year-old's wedding, but it seemed silly for us. Jane, being of sound mind, agreed, and allowed us to choose our own dresses as long as we stayed more or less within the color scheme.

Another less traditional outbreak of bridal tyranny occurred at the unusual wedding of my best friend Shelley. Shelley and Warren got married at the Grand Canyon, on a cliff at sunset overlooking the spectacular gorge. We were a small group, about 15 people. The morning of the wedding Shelley took a few of us out scouting for a good spot on the canyon rim for the ceremony. There were many beautiful spots, but Shelley became slightly obsessive when she started leading us up slippery narrow ledges and down tiny trails in search of a perfect one. After about 45 minutes of this, we started complaining, especially since none of us were planning to wear hiking boots to the wedding. But she was determined to search until she found what she wanted. We'd point out this spot and that, she'd snap at us about how wrong it was, and things were starting to get ugly, so we finally backed off and just enjoyed the view while she did her thing. Finally she settled on a place, and gradually returned to her normal state of mind over the next couple of hours.

The wedding turned out great, and even though a bank of dark clouds rolled in and rain fell for about 10 minutes, it was a spectacular setting, and Shelley & Warren were ecstatic. I even published a story about it in the wedding magazine, with photos and everything.

Location, Location, Location

"For those of us who came of age in the 1960's and 70's, nature weddings -- in rugged and unusual outdoor environments -- were the flavor of the week. It's likely that many of us have attended at least one wedding under a full moon in the forest, or on a deserted beach at sunset, and for those who preferred to live by common sense rather than tradition, sneakers and a warm jacket

replaced chiffon dresses and tuxedos as we trekked through mud and sand to share in the nuptial joy.

"Nature does more than provide a dramatic backdrop for a ceremony. It makes a profound statement about life and its cycles of birth, reproduction death and rebirth. When you superimpose a bride and groom over that background, you realize that marriages are part of a much larger plan than the one that focuses on what colors the bridesmaids will wear and who will escort Aunt Sara down the aisle. For some people, gathering friends and family in a church to witness your declaration of love makes for a perfect wedding. But for others, nature, in all its fierceness and enormity, is the true guest of honor."

The above is a quote from the article I wrote about Shelley and Warren's Grand Canyon wedding. Outdoor locations are wonderful, but if you're inviting a large group of people, you'll need to consider the comfort of elders, kids and others who may not be able to manage a hike down a canyon trail.

In 1974 I went to two memorable hippie weddings. One was held deep in the forest on the northern California commune where the brides and grooms lived (it was a double wedding). The event was beautiful and profound, but a real hassle when it came to carrying in food, tables and other necessities. The other -- my favorite wedding of all time -- was on a high cliff overlooking the sea. The guests gathered there, and watched the bride and groom arrive from across the grassy moors on a motorcycle, he driving and she on the back, her veil trailing in the wind behind her. After the ceremony, we all walked together back to the home of the couple, a few hundred yards from where the wedding had been. It was much easier having the reception in a place with running water.

In another example, Carl and Rhonda decided to get married at 6 am (in the morning!) on a deserted beach. There were two problems with this. One, many guests simply refused to show up at this outrageous hour, and two, the minister's voice, along with the voices of Carl and Rhonda, was inaudible against the sound of the crashing waves and the chilly wind. Be aware of problems like this. Nature is beautiful, but it can be cold and noisy.

The Content vs. the Form

While you may insist on a traditional white church wedding, it's important to know that you're allowed to improvise on the content of the ceremony. Consider a few alternatives, such as writing your own vows, having a talented friend sing a special song, including a reading of your favorite poetry, or involving selected friends and family in the ceremony by having them say a few words. This last idea is the one I like best, because a wedding, or a commitment ceremony, is about declaring your love to the world, and then taking your place in that world as a bonded couple. Why not include the world in the rites? Instead of facing the officiator, turn and face the audience to recite your lines. At the very least, face each other. I've seen many weddings in which the bride and groom stared into the face of the minister throughout the whole ceremony, and never looked at each other until the end. Deep unwavering eye contact between bride and groom should be *required*. If you can't look each other in eye, you shouldn't be getting married.

Keeping Yourself Sane

Wedding traditions, like all other traditions, are not set in cement, and there is no rule, law or cultural taboo against altering them slightly to fit your needs and your personality (unless you're deeply devoted to a particular religion or tradition that forbids you to improvise). So when planning a wedding, start by giving yourself permission to step outside convention and use your imagination. This event should be for the bride and groom, and no one else (though remember to respect other people's boundaries when it comes to choosing bridesmaid's gowns and other details that might enforce your will too strongly on others).

Parents and other family members may want to take charge, and there are sensitive emotional politics involved there (especially when the family is footing the bill). So set boundaries and state preferences right from the start by calling a meeting of all involved and laying your cards on the table about your vision of the event. Then let the negotiations begin.

A wedding requires the same consideration for the social comfort of the guests as any other party. While it's true that they're all there because of their love for you, they're still going to need help meeting and relating *to one another.* You (if you're the bride, groom or a closely involved family member) are going to be too distracted to manage the normal duties of a host, so I suggest appointing two or more "social ambassadors" to help out. You might ask some of the bridesmaids or ushers who have outgoing personalities to do this for you, or recruit other friends, especially those who will be attending the wedding unaccompanied. If you have it in your budget, you can hire a professional wedding coordinator who will assume this role. Some of his or her tasks might include:

- Greeting people at the door as they arrive.

- Acting as emcee from the stage at the reception.

- Table-hopping, introducing themselves and providing introductions for others.

- Facilitating activities, such as letting people know that it's time to move into an adjacent room for the cake-cutting.

- Music coordinator - maintaining communication with the band or emcee to handle special requests, channel information, schedule toasts & other presentations.

- Detail management - Handling the little hassles that occur, such as running out of white wine, deciding when it's time to cut the cake, handling the exchange of money with the hired help, and a thousand other unpredictable crises that a bride and groom should not have to be bothered with.

- Acting as your personal assistant and messenger. The band leader might want to know if you'd like them to stay an extra hour (for additional cost) or cut them loose at 11:00. Your assistant can relay messages like this back and forth, and act as your spokesperson. You might need to get a message to the kitchen, the valet parking guys, or the baby-sitter who's at home watching your kids. Your assistant can handle all this for you.

Low Cost
Wedding Agendas and Menus
by Kay Okrand

Kay Okrand is the owner of Memorable Occasions, a catering company in Van Nuys, California. In addition to being an expert on weddings (she catered mine), Kay offers consulting & event planning services, and conducts seminars on event planning and the catering business.

Kay believes that a wedding doesn't have to cost a fortune to be beautiful, memorable and fun. Here are some of her recommendations for low cost wedding alternatives:

As a guide, use these seven basic segments of the day and night in which weddings can be held. Following are suggested menus for each one:

Morning Wedding - 9 am - 12 noon.

A buffet breakfast or champagne brunch is lovely. You can serve Danish, croissants, muffins, fresh fruits of the season, bagels, breads and a coffee & tea bar.

Noon Wedding

Serve brunch or a buffet luncheon, but be sure to make it a full meal because it is lunch time and people will by hungry. Poached salmon, grilled chicken, salad bar, cold pastas.

Late Afternoon Wedding - 3 - 5 pm

Perfect for a simple champagne & cake reception. Add tea and coffee, possibly juices and mineral water. Can also serve a light buffet, champagne punch, tea sandwiches, fruit & fromage and other pre-dinner foods.

Cocktail Hour Wedding - 4 - 7 pm

Serve pre-dinner foods: cheese & crackers, champagne, cold cuts, tabouli salads, hummus & pita bread, chips & salsa, steamed dim sum, antipasto.

Early Dinner Wedding - 5 pm

This should always include dinner, which can be food stations, buffet of formal sit-down. Pasta and lasagna are affordable and can even be made by family and friends. Families can cook their ethnic specialties. Try a pasta bar with two sauces, two salads, breads, fresh fruits, cake & champagne.

Dinner Hour Wedding - 8 pm

It doesn't *have to* include dinner, but do serve heavy hors d oeuvres, carved meats and turkey, potato salad, pastas, appetizer trays and other things similar to the pre-dinner foods. Passed foods give you more control over how much people take, but have at least two table-top items available, such as cheeses & dips with crackers.

Dessert Only - 9 pm

For dessert-only receptions, mark on the invitation that's it's cake and champagne, so people will know that it's not a meal and they can plan to eat first. While cake and champagne may be sugar and alcohol heavy, its not a host's responsibility to adapt the menu for those who haven't eaten dinner. But do offer fruit and mineral water or sparkling cider or juice, coffee, tea, so there's something else to choose from.

10. The Caterer's Point of View

Pavilion Catering has been the in-house caterer for the Los Angeles Music Center for the past 17 years. The company has an exclusive agreement with the Music Center to serve as the official caterer for all events on site, including the world-famous Governors Ball -- the private party held each year after the Academy Awards. Pavilion caters the event every two out of three years.

Jeanne Anne O'Connor is the sales manager, and provides these useful insights:

Q. Describe an ideal room set up to encourage mingling.

A. In a private home a host should provide a choice of environments, such as indoor and outdoor, or different rooms for the party to move in and out of. One engagement party I attended in Denver was held in an old mansion with several rooms, and in each room the table settings were different because people were asked to bring in their own tableware. The cake was served in one room, champagne in another. It worked because it kept people moving. Sit down dinners also work well this way, if you can have tables in more than one room.

For standing receptions only, it's a good idea to have fewer chairs than people. A good ratio is one-third fewer chairs than guests. Food stations are better for mingling than a sit-down format. It has, in fact, become quite a trend for weddings.

Q. What are the most common mistakes made by hosts?

A. Seating too many people at a table. A 60 inch round table holds a maximum of 10. Smaller tables with fewer people work much better. Also, neglecting to plan a preliminary mingling period prior to seating at dinner or lunch events. Another common mistake is choosing tall centerpieces that block people's views of one another. Umbrella arrangements or a high bottleneck style with a spray of flowers overhead are preferable.

Q. What can a host do to improve conversation and create more fun?

A. The host should "table hop" to make introductions and keep conversation flowing. You can also appoint a friend as an "ambassador" who can walk around facilitating introductions.

It's important to provide something for guests to do other than sitting, chatting and eating. Hire a palm reader, cartoonist or magician to move from table to table. Think up games, contests and other activities. And there should be on-going entertainment from the podium or microphone, such as testimonials from friends about the guest of honor, presentation of awards, joke telling contests, etc.

One woman threw a party for her mother's 70th birthday, and hired a DJ who played big band music. Prior to the party, she asked guests to write down the name of their favorite song from the 30's and 40's, and a description of the memories the song evoked. These were read throughout the party whenever each of the songs were played.

Q. What's the best agenda for business party?

A. Pre-meal:
Allow 30-40 minutes of networking, with a cash bar. You can provide stations for appetizers to keep people moving. At check in, set up a networking game where people get stars or colored tags to identify them as new members of the group, VIPs or visitors, and urge the different colors to talk to each other. Give prizes for collecting the most business cards from people within each color code.

Seating:
Mix VIPs with newcomers and others. Designate "table leaders" to facilitate introductions at each table.

During the meal:
If there is a speaker or presentation, do it in short segments, which will allow people to eat and talk to each other between segments. Don't conduct a long presentation during a meal, because it will prevent table mates from talking to each other.

Q. What works for surprise parties?

A. Be sure to tell guests that they must arrive on time, to avoid running into the guest of honor during his or her arrival. Invite guests one hour earlier.

For example, at a retirement party for an important executive of a Fortune 500 company, his wife took him to the Music Center in formal attire ostensibly to see an opera. A limo delivered them to a VIP entrance in back, and they went up the VIP elevator to guarantee that they wouldn't run into guests who were arriving for the surprise party. Once the elevator landed on the party floor, all his friends were there.

Q. Any interesting stories about celebrity parties?

A. Celebrities are used to going to fancy affairs, so at their own personal parties, like birthdays anniversaries, they like to be more casual. At a party for the rock band ZZ Top we served ribs and spicy shrimp with piles of napkins because it was very messy, and everyone loved it because it was very casual... it was *homey*. Rock & roll people enjoy casual parties.

At a party for Bruce Springsteen there was a DJ who played oldies. We also brought in pinball machines for him, and did the same thing for The Who. People played basketball in the yard and played pinball inside. It was very casual and relaxed.

For Graham Nash's 40th birthday party, his wife asked all his friends to dress up as elderly people. Some of them had professional make-up done, so they were barely recognizable. They brought gifts related to aging, like hearing aids, vitamins and denture cream.

11. Surprise Party Tips

Everybody loves a surprise, right? Well before you make such a sweeping pronouncement, take a minute to consider some of the drawbacks in planning a surprise party. While surprise parties usually sound like a good idea at first, there are a few little things you need to watch out for, and this list will help you scan for them.

- Don't throw a surprise party for a divorced, separated or presently quarreling couple in the hopes of reconciling them. Unless of course both parties have consented to this, which is unlikely, and then it wouldn't be a surprise anyway.

- Always ask guests to arrive one hour before the guest of honor is due to arrive. You don't want the birthday boy pulling into his driveway to find a group of his friends walking toward his front door bearing gifts. It kind of ruins the surprise.

- Know in advance how the potential surprisee feels about surprise parties. If she's had a bad experience with it in the past, it might be best to forget the whole thing. The wife of a friend of mine threw her husband a huge surprise party at a nightclub in Los Angeles to celebrate a big business deal he'd made. She hired his favorite band and filled the room with all his friends. He was surprised all right, but the whole event made him very uncomfortable for some reason (a traumatic surprise party experience in his past perhaps?) and it resulted in a terrible rift between the couple, which lasted for weeks.

- Recruit accomplices. If you're planning a party for your boyfriend, make sure his co-workers, family or friends can help you out by making sure he's prepared to receive the surprise. For example, you don't want the party to occur on a night where he suddenly decides to work late. It helps to know that a co-worker will be at the office to talk him out of it.

- Be sure to hand-write on the invitation that it's a surprise. If this information isn't emphasized strongly enough, someone will inadvertently spill the beans.

- Make sure you designate a private phone number, office number or another trustworthy person to receive RSVPs and other inquiries.

12. An Expert Writes

Following is a letter I received from my good friend Matt Kramer, an entertainment industry entrepreneur who dabbles in about 12 other fields and has been to parties all over the world. In doing research for this book, I'd asked him for his thoughts on what makes a good party, and he responded by sending me this clever and informative letter. It was so thorough and descriptive that I decided to reprint it in its entirety.

Dear Terri:

Good parties I have known? One element I've noticed that always gives a party a sense of depth is to hold it in a place where guests can move in a circle. Your house has a perfect layout for this. One can wander from the living room into the dining room to the food table (generally the initial plot point of the evening) and then take a gander into the kitchen. By the time the guest has perused the kitchen, if he or she has not yet found any stimulating conversation, there are two choices; either into the back yard, or back into the living room to begin the circle over again. The interesting thing about this migratory pattern is that everyone's doing the same thing, so you get a chance to see each guest at least once. In the worst case, the guest can wander around four or five times before realizing that he is either bored or too panic-stricken to break the ice with a stranger and begin to enjoy himself. At this point, nothing much is going to help, and next time you'll know better than to invite him and put him through this torturous confrontation with his own sense of inadequacy.

By establishing a tradition, like your yearly music jam session, you give guests some concrete choices: to either perform or be members of the audience. Two kinds of personalities are served in this case; the frustrated artist who has no venue can now have a captive audience, while the bored/panicked guest can now look interested in something while fumbling for an inspiring comment to make to the bored/panicked (but attractive) guest sitting nearby.

I think a good party is one in which there is either a common theme or purpose for gathering, or the host provides a combination of activities or options to keep peoples' attention. If the guests respond or move the party in a different direction, the host needs to be resilient and move with the whims of the guests.

I once gave a party in which I invited about 40 of my favorite people. The invitations included a one-paragraph description of ever person on the guest list. I remember one of the guests lived in Mexico City and I was so honored that she flew up to attend the party. People came specifically looking to meet others whose descriptions they liked! It was one of the best parties I ever created, and as I think about it now, I don't think I've thrown as successful a party since. I don't know if I could top that one, and besides, I don't have a house where people can move around in a circle.

Matt

13. The Perfect Party Checklist

As an overview, after you've considered the menu, the theme and the visual elements of your party, take a look at the *emotional* needs of your guests. You might find this checklist useful in helping you to manage the mingling:

The Guest List

- In a group of 10 or more, mix and match! Invite people with common interests of course, but avoid having a room that includes only golf-playing heart surgeons. An evening of shop-talk can be miserable for outsiders, and it keeps the insiders from experiencing new people and new ideas. For the sake of interesting social texture, add artists, firefighters, librarians, unemployed friends and people of an opposing political bent. Mix singles with couples, and consider a wide age span (in a large enough group, people in their twenties can mix happily with people in their sixties).

- When people begin calling to RSVP, give them an idea of what type of crowd you expect. Inform your friends in advance about specific individuals they may wish to meet at the party, and promise to provide introductions.

- Be aware of how important it is for you to expand your circle of friends, and make it a rule to always bring new acquaintances into the fold. Invite people you hardly know but would like to know better.

- Don't get hung up on people's personal politics. If you want to invite two feuding family members, or two members of a now-defunct couple, go ahead and issue the invitation, and allow them to be responsible for their own dramas. You might just end up being a catalyst for change! Also, respect the fact that both individuals have a right to decline your invitation because of their situation, and don't hold it against them.

Food and Drink

- Poorly chosen food can spell disaster, not to mention make people sick. Serving only junk food, solely meat-based dishes or just cake & champagne at an event where people need more sustenance will alienate at least half of your guests. Offer a balance of sensible and extravagant foods.

- Always include both alcoholic and non-alcoholic beverages, unless your party is a gathering of recovering alcoholics. And make sure you have enough of everything! If you run out, be prepared to go (or send someone) to the store.

- Provide comfortable eating and drinking spaces. There's nothing worse than standing on your feet balancing a plate of food and a wine glass while reaching into your pocket for a business card.

- Some hosts won't serve red wine or other dark-colored beverages because they're afraid of spills that might stain the carpet. As a red wine lover, I find this rather irritating. Instead, roll up the expensive Persian rug and make sure you have some cleaning solvents on hand in case of accidents.

- Get help! If you're doing all the cooking yourself, don't hesitate to ask a friend to help or to contribute (or just make it a pot luck).

- Remember to serve something that will appeal to kids, vegetarians, people from other cultures, or people with special dietary needs.

Activities and Entertainment

- Never throw a group of people together with no focus, agenda or purpose and expect them to fend for themselves.

- Plan an activity to serve as a central focus for everyone, such as a presentation for the guest of honor, party games (with prizes), or a participatory activity like standing around the piano singing oldies. If needed, hire a piano player or other entertainment. If you're not comfortable in the role of organizer, enlist the help of a friend who is.

- Avoid excessively loud music that forces people to shout in order to be heard(unless you're all under 25). If you're planning to have recorded music playing throughout the entire party, make sure to provide quiet areas where people can go to talk. If there is a live band, locate it away from conversation areas. Provide a dance floor if at all possible (it's the best ice breaker in the world). If you can afford it, hire a professional dancing teacher to give group lessons for 30-45 minutes.

- Don't invent stringent party themes that impose on people's identities (avoid asking people to dress as their favorite vegetable).

- Background music should be varied, not just to please different musical palates, but to create shifts in the energy. Mix rock & roll, 40s standards, opera and world music on your CD player, push the "random play" button, and watch what happens. It also helps to select music in advance that will create different moods for different phases of the party, or ask friends to bring interesting tapes or CDs to share.

- Hire or designate an emcee for the party. This idea may seem a bit controlling, but don't knock it 'till you've tried it. Look at what wedding and Bar Mitzvah bandleaders do. What would these events be like if they didn't invite the Bar Mitzvah boy's family to the stage to light the candles, or if the bride and groom didn't steal the show with their romantic first dance as a married couple? If you have a friend who's got a funny, outgoing personality and loves to perform (we all know someone like that), ask him to emcee your next party, and see what happens.

- Another music note: Sometimes it's OK to have no music at all. If there's a stimulating conversation going on at an intimate dinner party, music of any kind has the potential to be a distraction.

- Provide diversions for children. Toys & games, a separate room where they can play and make noise, nutritious foods that kids enjoy, videos on a tv in the den, or a hired baby sitter will make things easier for everybody (including the kids!).

Making People Comfortable

- Introduce people to one another by giving more information than simply their names ("Ramon, this is Jim. He runs a non-profit association for AIDS research and has a seven year-old son. Jim, Ramon's a single father who just moved here from Atlanta.").

- Assign tasks to guests who ask for them (it makes them feel useful, especially if they're shy). It's also a great way to rescue someone who seems lost, lonely or uncomfortable.

- Take an active role in bringing people together. Make a point of introducing people to others whom they might want to know (you can never do too much of this).

- Let your house look lived-in and comfortable. If it's too organized, sparkling clean and filled with expensive antiques and delicate surfaces, people will feel stiff and unsure about where to put their drinks and where to sit. You don't want people walking on eggshells for fear of dirtying or breaking something.

- Make creature comforts easily accessible. In the guest bathroom, place useful items like hand lotion, tissues, tampons, needle & thread, Q-tips, dental floss, contact lens cleaner, breath mints, aspirins and other amenities where guests can find them easily without having to ask (or worse, without having to rummage through your cabinets!)

- Make a separate room available for people who want to have private conversations or watch the game on TV (an incredibly rude thing to do, unless they've been invited specifically or this purpose. However, you may wish to accommodate sports fanatics in this way if you don't mind losing them for the rest of the party).

Physical Well-Being, Convenience and Safety

- Stage your party in as many varied spaces as possible -- drinks in one area, food in another, party games in another -- to keep people moving. It helps to provide slightly fewer chairs than people for the same reason.

- Be sure lighting, air circulation, sound levels and room temperatures are comfortable.

- Keep boisterous pets outside or in another room.

- Provide activities to keep children occupied.

- Begin your party at a reasonable hour! Don't have a wine tasting party in your downtown office at 4 pm on a weekday, forcing your guests to drive home in rush hour traffic...drunk. A sunrise wedding on the beach in the middle of winter is lovely, but can be a real inconvenience for your friends.

- Know the phone number of your local cab company, or have other driving alternatives available for inebriated guests.

- Let your neighbors know you'll be having a party (it may make them think twice before calling the police if you get too noisy). Better yet, invite them! It's good for community relations.

- Make sure extension cords, electric wires, heavy or sharp objects and other dangers are out of the way. Put floormats or Astroturf on slippery outdoor areas during rain or pool parties. Make sure children are kept out of danger and properly supervised. In other words, avoid tragedies and lawsuits.

- Have an earthquake or fire evacuation plan.

- Have insurance.

Keeping Yourself Sane

- Absolutely, without fail, hire help for serving, clean-up or child care! Your job is to entertain, bring people together, and have a good time... not to sweat, schlep and serve. If you can't afford professional help, use a neighborhood teenager for minimum wage, or a good friend who owes you a favor.

- Dress for comfort, not for speed. You'll be on your feet a lot, so if high heels are going to kill you, forget them.

- Don't burn yourself out. Make a point of sitting down as often as possible. Even though you need to be moving around taking care of people, you're allowed to sit and rest occasionally. As the host, people will come to you for conversation, so it's entirely feasible to "hold court" in your favorite chair for breather here and there.

- Allow people to make themselves at home. Show them where the refrigerator is, where things are at the bar and other ways in which they can serve themselves. You'll not only save wear and tear on yourself, but you'll create a more relaxed atmosphere for your friends.

- Pace your drinking and eating. Try to eat something substantial before the party begins so that you're not operating on an empty stomach. The host of a large party often gets too busy to sit down and eat. And drink alcoholic beverages slowly and carefully, interspersed with glasses of water, to keep your energy level up.

- If you have children, hire a baby sitter to entertain them, feed them and put them to bed when the time comes.

- Although it may be bad for the landfill, go ahead and use plastic or paper plates, glasses and tableware to your heart's desire. Even for a buffet dinner, if it's an informal party for a large group and you buy high quality plastic, nobody will mind.

- Keep waste baskets stationed here and there to subtly encourage people to dispose of their own used plates, cups, napkins, etc.

- Remember to have fun!

Index